All About AFL

Amy Hunter

Contents

The Best Game in the World! 2

What Is AFL? 6

Teams and Players 8

Playing the Game 10

Footballers 12

Umpires and Coaches 14

That Day in September 16

The Best of the Best! 18

You Can Play Footy! 20

Fantastic Footy Facts! 22

Glossary 24

The Best Game in the World!

The players are ready.
The football is bounced.
The crowd cheers ...
and the game starts!

There is no game in the world like AFL football. Football players have to:

- kick
- **handball**
- **mark**
- run!

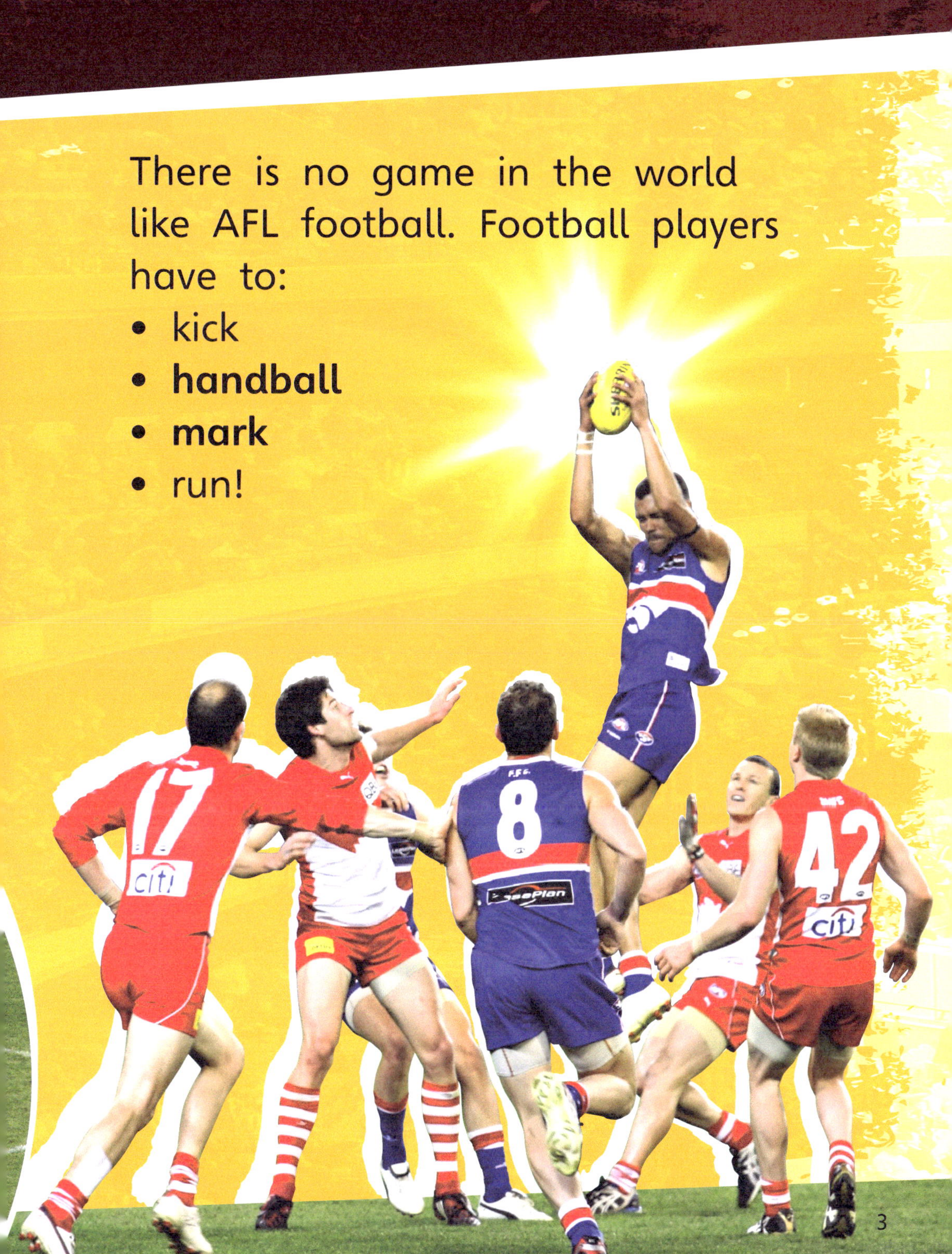

Lots of people have a favourite team that they **barrack** for. Lots of people play football too!

What footy team do you barrack for?

There might be some things about footy that you do not know. So, put on your footy beanie, grab a meat pie and read on ...

What Is AFL?

The AFL is the **A**ustralian **F**ootball **League.** AFL football is played in most states in Australia.

Australian Rules football began in 1897. It is the biggest sporting **competition** in Australia!

an Australian Rules football match, 1920

Teams and Players

There are 16 teams in the AFL. Each team has a **captain**. The captain leads the team.

There are 18 players in each team, with four extra players. When the players on the field need a rest, they swap with the extra players.

Fremantle Dockers

The AFL Teams

Team	State	Nickname	Colours
Adelaide	South Australia	The Crows	
Brisbane	Queensland	The Lions	
Carlton	Victoria	The Blues	
Collingwood	Victoria	The Magpies	
Essendon	Victoria	The Bombers	
Fremantle	Western Australia	The Dockers	
Geelong	Victoria	The Cats	
Hawthorn	Victoria	The Hawks	
Melbourne	Victoria	The Demons	
North Melbourne	Victoria	The Kangaroos	
Port Adelaide	South Australia	The Power	
Richmond	Victoria	The Tigers	
St Kilda	Victoria	The Saints	
Sydney	New South Wales	The Swans	
West Coast	Western Australia	The Eagles	
Western Bulldogs	Victoria	The Bulldogs	

Playing the Game

The footballers play in special places on the field. Some players kick goals. Other players stop the other team from kicking goals!

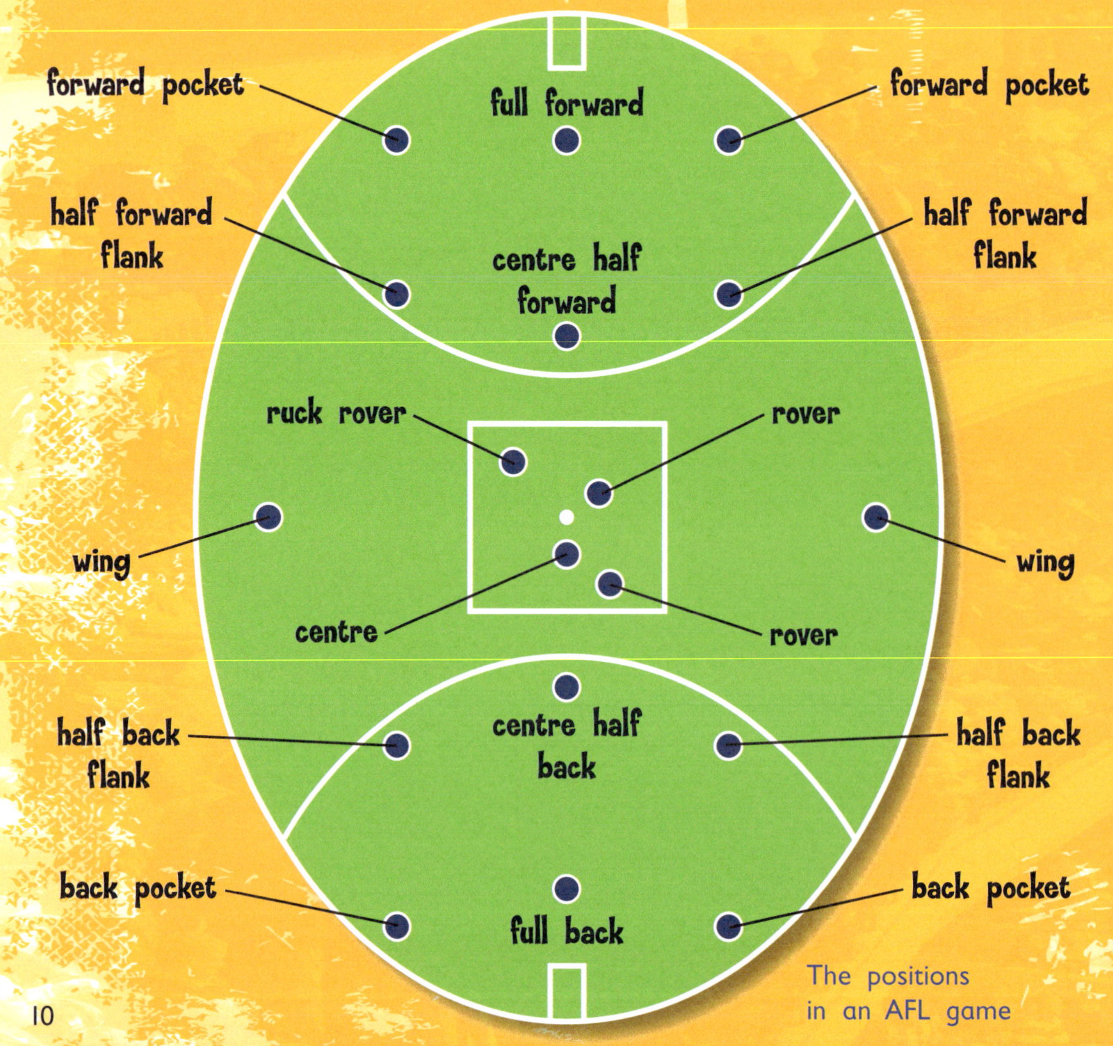

The positions in an AFL game

There are four parts in a football game. Each part is about 20 minutes long. At the end of the game, the team with the biggest **score** wins!

Collingwood	12	11	83
Adelaide	11	12	78

If the ball is kicked through the tall posts it is a goal. A goal is six points.

If the ball is kicked through the tall and the short post, it is one point.

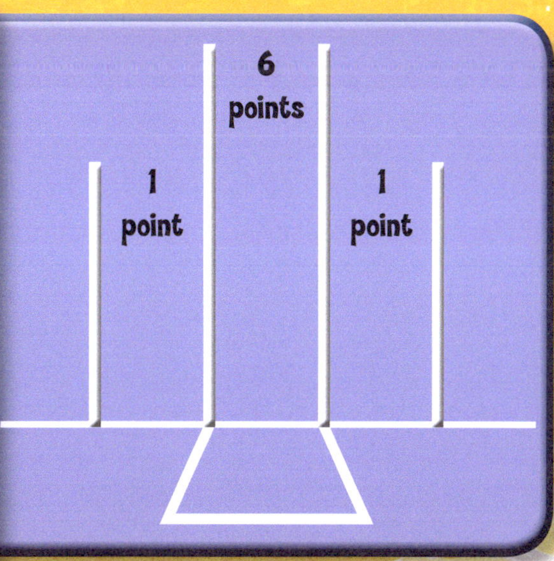

Footballers

Footballers have to be very fit! They have to:

- handball the ball to another player
- mark the ball
- run fast
- kick the ball a long way

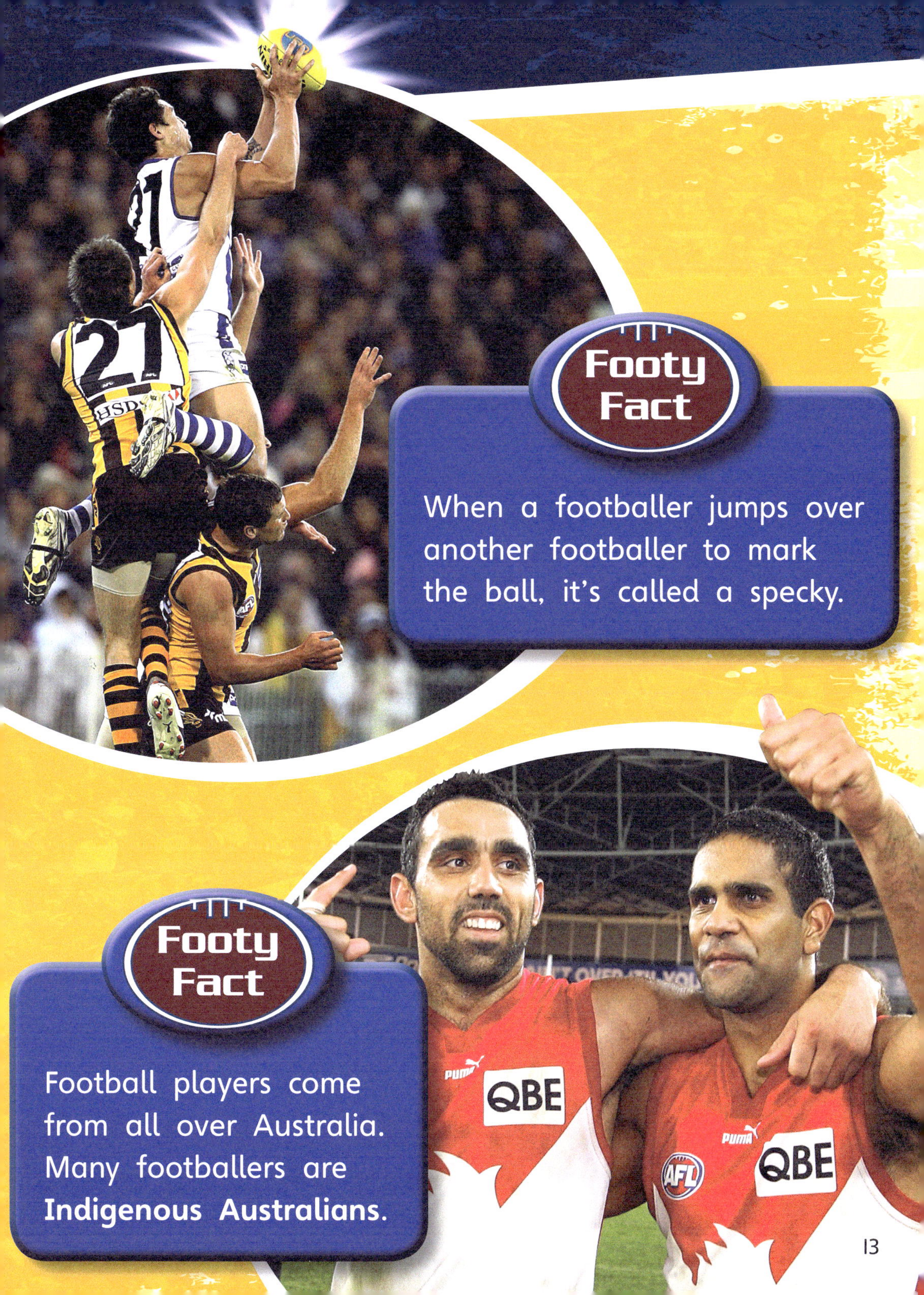

Footy Fact

When a footballer jumps over another footballer to mark the ball, it's called a specky.

Footy Fact

Football players come from all over Australia. Many footballers are **Indigenous Australians.**

Umpires and Coaches

You can't have a football game without an umpire. Umpires make all the players play by the rules.

All football teams need a coach. A coach helps the players keep fit and play better.

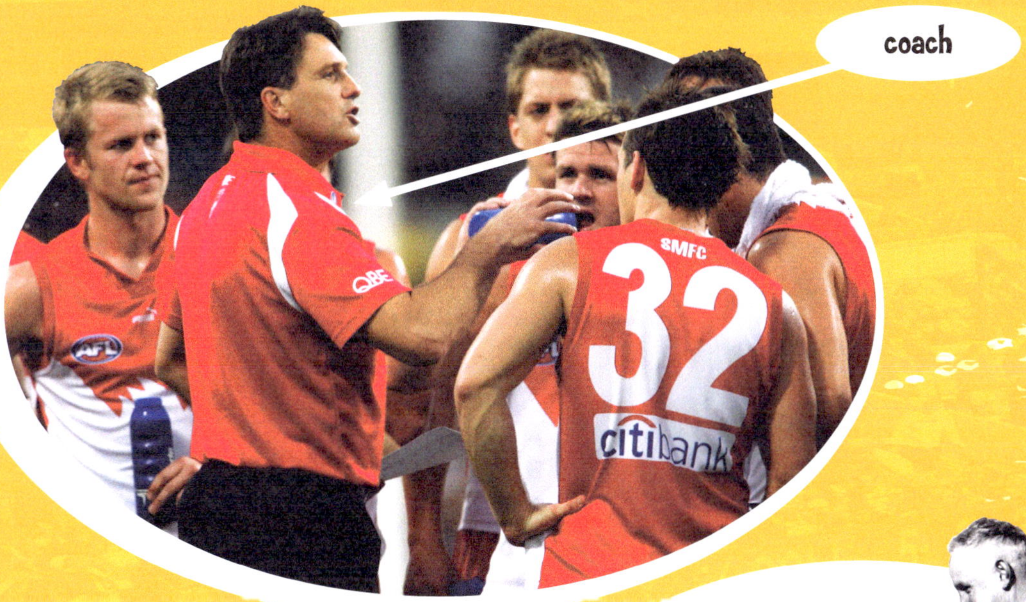

coach

Jock McHale has coached the most games of AFL. He coached 714 games for Collingwood.

That Day in September

In September, the two best AFL teams play in the Grand Final. A grand final is held every year.

The team who wins the Grand Final is called the **premiership** team. They are given a cup and flag.

Geelong Cats

Footy Fact

Essendon and Carlton have won the most AFL premierships – 16 each!

The Best of the Best!

Each year the best player in the AFL is given a medal. This is called the Brownlow Medal. The winner is chosen by the umpires.

Gary Ablett Jr has won a Brownlow Medal.

Meet Adam Goodes

One of the best AFL players is Adam Goodes, an Indigenous Australian. He won the Brownlow Medal in 2003 and 2006.

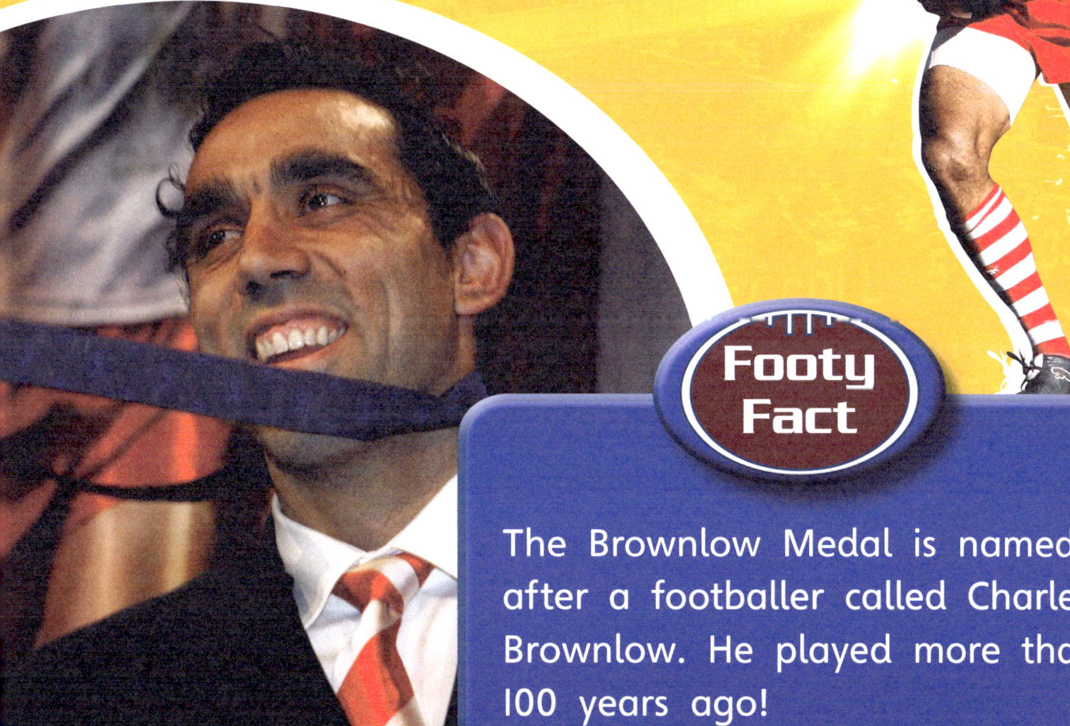

Footy Fact

The Brownlow Medal is named after a footballer called Charles Brownlow. He played more than 100 years ago!

You Can Play Footy!

If you want to play like an AFL footballer, you can!

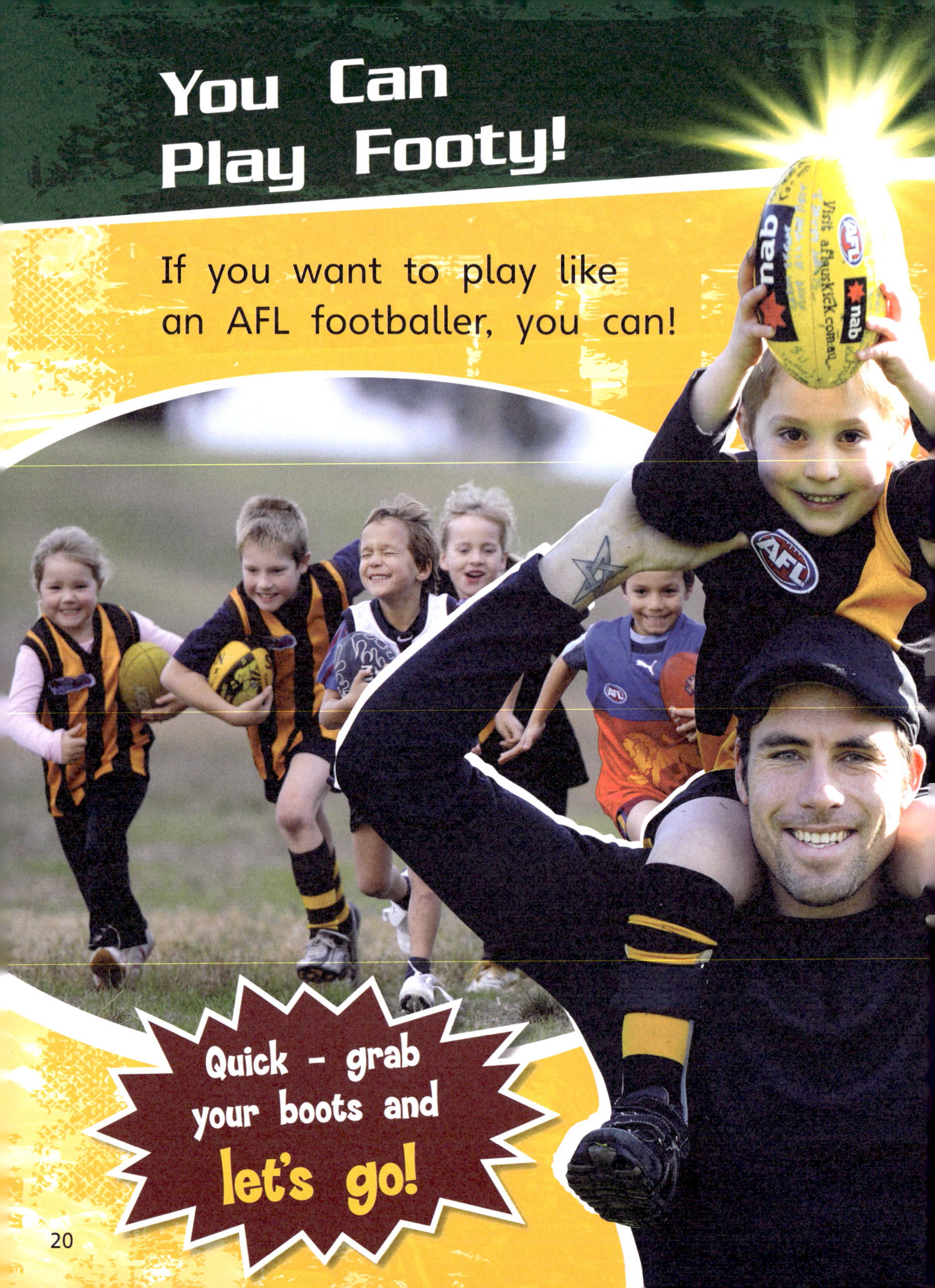

At **Auskick** you learn how to:

- kick
- handball
- mark
- play in a game.

One day, you could be playing in the AFL too!

Fantastic Footy Facts!

The Most Goals in a Game

Fred Fanning kicked 18 goals for Melbourne against St Kilda, in 1947.

The Most Goals by a Footballer

Tony Lockett has kicked the most goals – 1360 goals.

The Most Games by a Footballer

Michael Tuck played 426 games.

The Longest Kick

The longest kick ever in the AFL was 98.5 metres!

Glossary

Auskick	a coaching program where children learn the skills to play Australian Rules
Australian Rules	the football game played by AFL teams
barrack	to go for a team
captain	the leader of a team
competition	a game that a person or team wins
handball	to hold the football in one hand and hit it with the fist of the other hand
Indigenous Australians	Australian Aboriginal and Torres Strait Islander people
league	a group of sporting teams
mark	to catch the football
premiership	a sports prize
score	the total number of points